This book belongs to:

Just for the

BRIDE

p

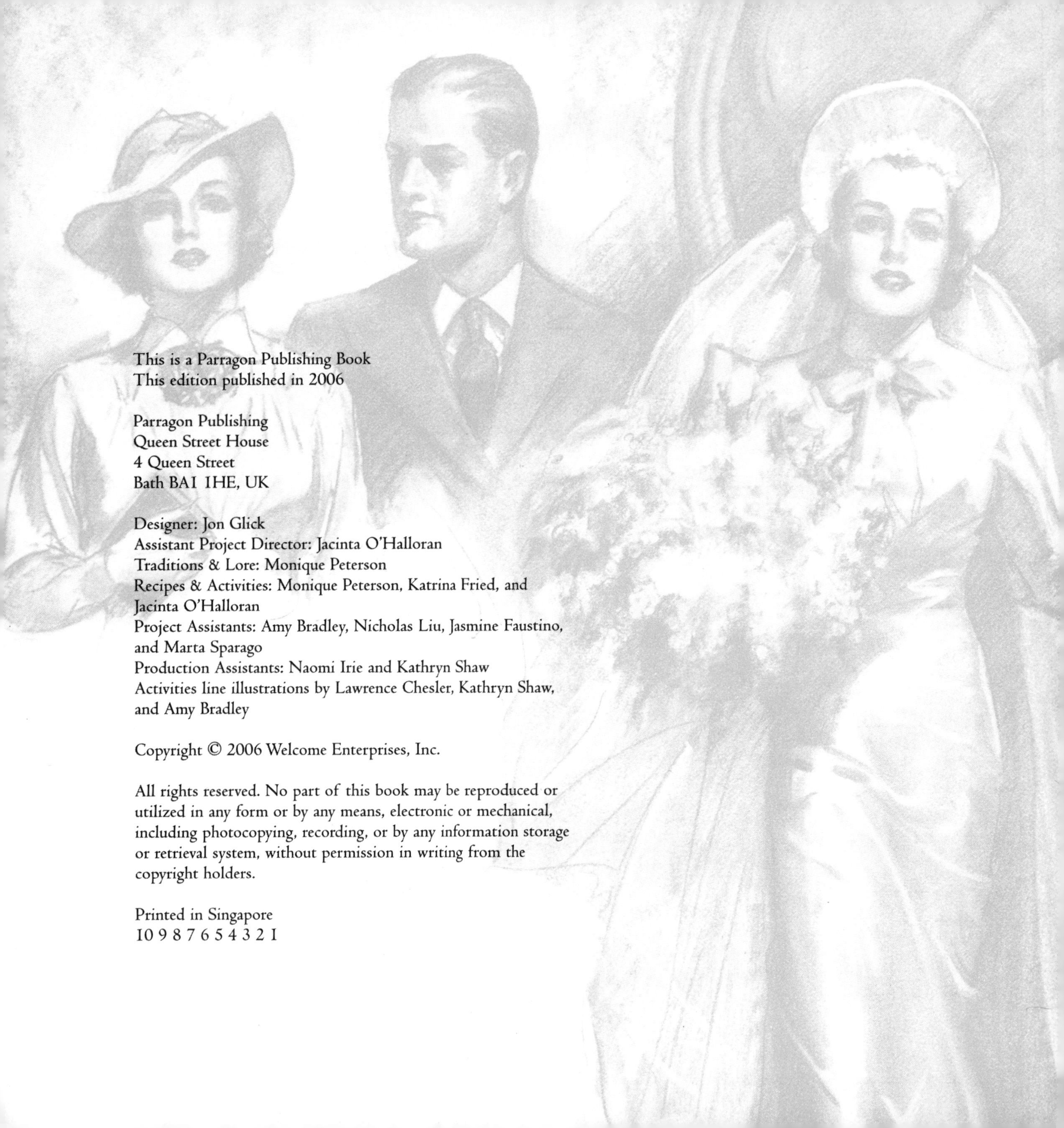

This is a Parragon Publishing Book
This edition published in 2006

Parragon Publishing
Queen Street House
4 Queen Street
Bath BA1 1HE, UK

Designer: Jon Glick
Assistant Project Director: Jacinta O'Halloran
Traditions & Lore: Monique Peterson
Recipes & Activities: Monique Peterson, Katrina Fried, and
Jacinta O'Halloran
Project Assistants: Amy Bradley, Nicholas Liu, Jasmine Faustino,
and Marta Sparago
Production Assistants: Naomi Irie and Kathryn Shaw
Activities line illustrations by Lawrence Chesler, Kathryn Shaw,
and Amy Bradley

Printed in Singapore
10 9 8 7 6 5 4 3 2 1

The secret of a
happy marriage
remains a secret.

HENNY YOUNGMAN

TABLE OF CONTENTS

TRADITIONS & LORE

A MATCH MADE IN HEAVEN 16

ALWAYS A BRIDESMAID 72

DIAMONDS ARE A GIRL'S BEST FRIEND 42

HE LOVES ME, HE LOVES ME NOT 8

MARRY WHEN THE SUN DOTH SHINE 90

PREPARING THE BRIDE 86

SAY YOU'LL BE MINE 24

SHOWERING THE BRIDE 56

SOMETHING OLD SOMETHING NEW 66

THIS RING IS ROUND 34

READINGS & POETRY

A ROOM WITH A VIEW *E.M. Forster* 71

HOPEFUL PROPOSAL TO A YOUNG LADY
OF THE VILLAGE *Simon Fallowfield* 21

GRANDMOTHER'S QUILT *Annie F.S. Beard* 61

MARRY WHEN THE YEAR IS NEW 48

POEM XIII *James Joyce* 85

THE PASSIONATE SHEPHERD TO HIS LOVE
Christopher Marlowe 32

TO JULIA *Robert Herrick* 40

TO MY DEAR AND LOVING HUSBAND
Anne Bradstreet 31

ACTIVITIES & RECIPES

ATTENDANT GIFTS 76

GROOM'S GIFT: THE BOOK OF US 50

THE PAMPERED BRIDE 93

BRIDAL TEA PARTY 78

ENGAGEMENT COCKTAIL PARTY 45

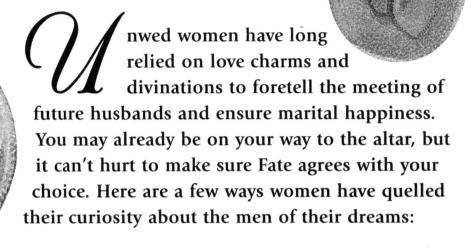

*U*nwed women have long relied on love charms and divinations to foretell the meeting of future husbands and ensure marital happiness. You may already be on your way to the altar, but it can't hurt to make sure Fate agrees with your choice. Here are a few ways women have quelled their curiosity about the men of their dreams:

He loves me, he loves me not . . .

❧ ON CHRISTMAS EVE, stand before the fireplace and gaze into the flames to see the image of your future husband.

❧ IF YOU LOVE A MAN and want to know if he will propose, throw a nut into the fire and say his name. If the nut jumps, you'll marry. If the nut doesn't move, the relationship will have no spark.

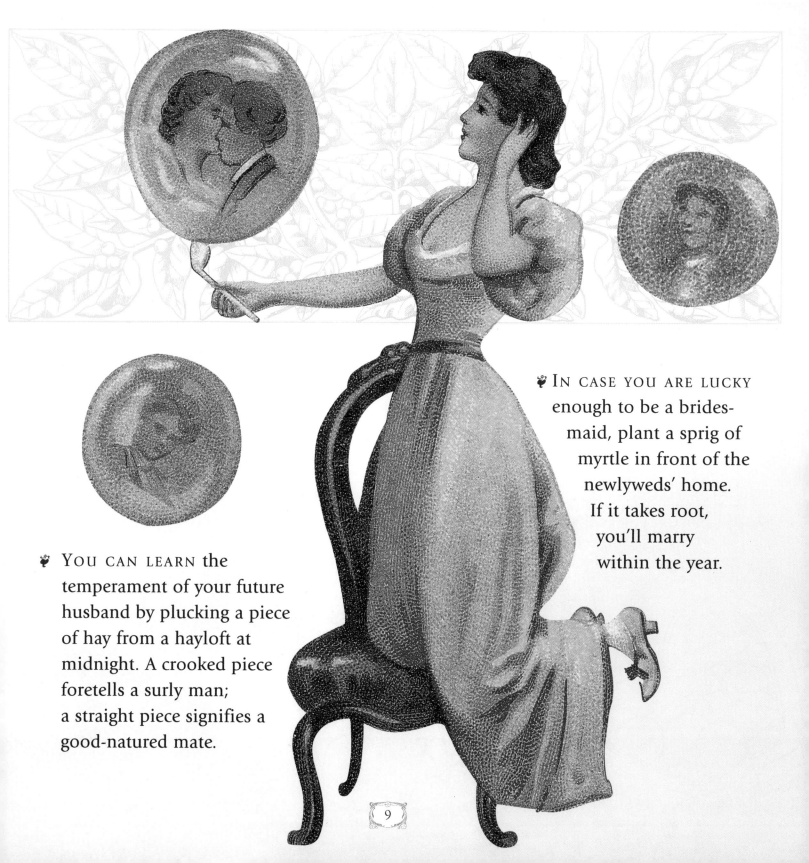

✿ IN CASE YOU ARE LUCKY
enough to be a brides-
maid, plant a sprig of
myrtle in front of the
newlyweds' home.
If it takes root,
you'll marry
within the year.

✿ YOU CAN LEARN the
temperament of your future
husband by plucking a piece
of hay from a hayloft at
midnight. A crooked piece
foretells a surly man;
a straight piece signifies a
good-natured mate.

PEEL AN APPLE in a single strip and toss the peel over your left shoulder. The shape of the peel will reveal the first letter of the name of your spouse to be.

🌸 Or pluck some wild daisies from a nearby field and put the roots under your pillow to dream of your groom.

🌸 On All Hallows Eve, brush your hair three times in front of a mirror. If you glimpse a man standing behind you, wedding bells will ring before the year is through.

🌸 When attending a wedding, be sure to take a piece of groom's cake home and put it under your pillow. That night the face of your future husband will appear in your dreams.

🌸 If that doesn't work, soak your shoelaces in water until they're saturated. Then throw them against the wall to see the initials of your soon-to-be betrothed.

I will tell you the real secret of how to stay married. Keep the cave clean. They want the cave clean and spotless. Air-conditioned, if possible. Sharpen his spear, and stick it in his hand when he goes out in the morning to spear that bear; and when the bear chases him, console him when he comes home at night, and tell him what a big man he is, and then hide the spear so he doesn't fall over it and stab himself…

JEROME CHODOROV AND JOSEPH FIELDS

If ever two were one, then surely we.
If ever man were loved by wife, then thee;
If ever wife was happy in a man,
Compare with me ye women if you can.
I prize thy love more than whole mines of gold,
Or all the riches that the East doth hold.
My love is such that rivers cannot quench,
Nor ought but love from thee, give recompence.
Thy love is such I can no way repay,
The heavens reward thee manifold I pray.
Then while we live, in love lets so persevere,
That when we live no more, we may live ever.

TO MY DEAR AND LOVING HUSBAND
Anne Bradstreet

For ages people who've hardly known each other, let alone come to love each other, have united through the divine wisdom of match-makers and fortune-tellers. Such bonds cement families, strengthen clans, and in the case of royal marriages, seal political contracts. If a good match can be foretold in the stars, all the better.

A match made in heaven

ACCORDING TO CHINESE LORE, the gods unite each couple at birth with an invisible red cord. In time, the cord grows shorter, drawing the pair together. The pivotal role of the matchmaker is to help these predestined people find each other, according to the 3,000-year-old practice of astrology. The matchmaker evaluates a possible union on the principals of the Eight Characters or Four Pillars. She writes down characters identifying the birth hour, day, month, and year of the prospective bride and groom on rice paper. According to some practices, if the characters are lucky and if nothing bad happens in three days, the marriage can be considered a good match.

When the time comes, the matchmaker hosts a betrothal tea for the groom and his parents. The prospective bride serves the tea. If the groom wishes to pursue marriage, he will place an embroidered red satchel on his saucer. The bride may accept his offer by taking the bag. If she is not interested, she will have politely left the room before the groom has an opportunity to show his interest.

A family starts with a young man falling in love with a girl. No superior alternative has been found.

WINSTON CHURCHILL

My Dear Miss,

I now take up my pen to write to you hoping these few lines will find you well as it leaves me at present Thank God for it. You will perhaps be surprised that I should make so bold as to write to you who is such a lady and I hope you will not be vex at me for it. I hardly dare say what I want, I am so timid about ladies, and my heart trimmels like a hespin. But I once seed in a book that faint heart never won fair lady, so here goes.

HOPEFUL PROPOSAL TO A YOUNG LADY OF THE VILLAGE

A REAL PROPOSAL LETTER
BY SIMON FALLOWFIELD

I am a farmer in a small way and my age is rather more than forty years and my mother lives with me and keeps my house, and she has been very poorly lately and cannot stir about much and I think I should be more comfortabler with a wife.

I have had my eye on you a long time and I think you are a very nice young woman and one that would make me happy if only you think so. We keep a servant girl to milk three kye and do the work in the house, and she goes on a bit in the summer to gadder wickens and she snags a few of turnips in the back kend. I do a piece of work on the farm myself and attends Pately Market, and I sometimes show a few sheep and I feeds between 3 & 4 pigs agen Christmas, and the same is very useful in the house to make pies and cakes and so forth, and I sells the hams to help pay for the barley meal.

I have about 73 pund in Naisbro Bank and we have a nice little parlour downstairs with a blue carpet, and an oven on the side of the fireplace and the old woman on the other side smoking. The Golden Rules claimed up on the walls above the long settle, and you could sit all day in the easy chair and knit and mend my kytles and leggums, and you could make the tea ready agin I come in, and you could make butter for Pately Market, and I would drive you to church every Sunday in the spring cart, and I would do all that bees in my power to make you happy. So I hope to hear from you. I am in desprit and Yurnest, and will marry you at May Day, or if my mother dies afore I shall want you afore. If only you will accept of me, my dear, we could be very happy together.

I hope you will let me know your mind by return of post, and if you are favourable I will come up to scratch. So no more at present from your well-wisher and true love—
    Simon Fallowfield

P.S. I hope you will say nothing about this. If you will not accept of me I have another very nice woman in my eye, and I think I shall marry her if you do not accept of me, but I thought you would suit me mother better, she being very crusty at times. So I tell you now before you come, she will be Maister.

THIS PROPOSAL WAS REFUSED BY MARY FOSTER,
THE LOCAL BEAUTY OF MIDDLEMOOR, PATELY BRIDGE, IN YORKSHIRE.

My most brilliant achievement was my ability to be able to persuade my wife to marry me.
WINSTON CHURCHILL.

Say you'll be mine

A candlelight dinner for two; a walk in the park hand in hand; a delivery of long-stemmed red roses. Ah, sweet romance! Dating customs of love-smitten men have ranged from the boisterous to the sublime— and have been, in some cases, less than virtuous! While your wedding may signify the end of courtship, it certainly does not mean the death of romance. Find inspiration in the following wooing traditions and keep your marriage full of passion.

THE ART OF SHOWERING one's true love with poems and serenades did not fade with Romeo and Juliet. Affection-seeking gentlemen in Spain, Brazil, and the Philippines still take this tradition very seriously. They hope to win the hearts of their beloved with verses they've composed themselves. Often they'll invite a group of friends to accompany them with musical instruments while they sing and dance until the wee hours of the morning.

IN MID-TWENTIETH-CENTURY AMERICA, the custom of dating involved time spent together on the porch swing or going to a drive-in movie. But during colonial times, couples courted between the sheets! English and Dutch emigrants from rural communities introduced this custom, called bundling, which was touted as a way to save on heating costs. Families permitted wooing couples to get to know each other—fully or partially dressed—in bed. A "bundling board" placed in the bed was supposed to separate the lovebirds and keep them chaste. Preventive measures weren't always failsafe, however, resulting in more than one pregnant bride at the altar....

HOW DOES A WOMAN SHOW that her heart belongs to someone? By spooning with her sweetheart, of course. What has come to be known as necking or snuggling got its start from an old Welsh custom. A man would woo his beloved with an elaborately carved wooden spoon. If she accepted his affections, she would attach it to a ribbon and wear it around her neck as a sign of betrothal.

IN RURAL POLAND, a man might show his feelings for a woman by visiting her and inquiring about purchasing a horse. If, during their conversation, he reveals a bottle of vodka wrapped in red ribbons and flowers, she'll know the visit has nothing to do with her horse. Instead of asking for her hand in marriage, he'll simply ask for a glass. If she is ready to be his bride, she'll return with glasses and her family to celebrate their betrothal.

In many African villages, courtship is not between two people, but between two families. If a prospective suitor wishes to inquire about a certain unwed female, he might send his mother, aunt, or other married female relative to knock on her family's door. She asks to arrange a meeting of family members and village elders. The prospective suitor will bring gifts of money, grain, produce, and livestock to show his ability to provide for his new bride and future family.

War of the Posies

In England, suitors were mad about flowers, especially during Victorian times, when virtually everything that bloomed carried a special symbolism. When a young man wished to gain the affection of a certain young woman, he would send her posies that held secret messages. She would reply in kind with specific flowers that would either welcome or shun his attentions. Here's a sampling of petal lore:

Ambrosia— "Love returned"

Burdock— "Touch me not"

Camellia— "You are perfected loveliness"

Currant— "Thy frown will kill me"

Daffodil— "Unrequited love"

Narcissus— "Uncertainty"

Pansies— "Think of me"

Peach blossoms— "Am I your captive?"

Pink rose— "Our love is perfect happiness"

Ranunculus— "You are radiant with charm"

Red columbine— "Anxious and trembling"

Wild daisy— "I will think of it"

I go about murmuring, 'I have made that dignified girl commit herself, I have, I have,' and then I vault over the sofa with exultation.

WALTER BAGEHOT
(MARRIED HIS LOVE ELIZABETH WILSON IN 1858)

Do you  all for me,

and my Love is as soft

as an   For you

          Hair   and

of my eye, so if we

anyhow, for I know we w

for my heart  for you

as a  but as strong

are a  with your

nose. You are the

then  marry,

uld make a happy

Come live with me and be my love,
And we will all the pleasures prove
That hills and valleys, dales and fields
And all the craggy mountains yields.

There we will sit upon the rocks
And see the shepherds feed their flocks,
By shallow rivers to whose falls
Melodious birds sing madrigals.

And I will make thee beds of roses
With a thousand fragrant posies,
A cap of flowers and a kirtle
Embroidered all with leaves of myrtle.

A gown made of the finest wool
Which from our pretty lambs we pull;
Fair lined slippers for the cold,
With buckles of the purest gold;

A belt of straw and ivy buds,
With coral clasps and amber studs:
And if these pleasures may thee move,
Come live with me and be my love.

The shepherds' swains shall dance
  and sing
For thy delight each May morning:
If these delights thy mind may move,
Then live with me and be my love.

THE PASSIONATE SHEPHERD
TO HIS LOVE

Christopher Marlowe

You're engaged! It's unmistakable: Friends and strangers alike know it's official when they see an engagement ring on your finger. But how did the ring become a symbol of marital unity?

This ring is round and hath no end

IN ANCIENT ROME, husbands promised commitment to their wives with rings made of iron. Those too poor to afford a ring would seal their engagement with the loop of a door key to the new marital home. Some of the earliest rings were not metal at all, but made of woven grasses or leather. Others were carved out of ivory or bone. In A.D. 860, Pope Nicholas I decreed a new mandate for the Catholic world to ensure that engagements would be binding: From then on, the ring was not only a requirement for nuptial intent but should be made of a valuable metal, preferably gold.

ANCIENT EGYPTIANS BELIEVED the ring, a perfect circle, represented a supernatural link to eternal love shared by two people. This is just one of the many shades of cultural meaning that rings have had throughout the history of marriage.

So is my love unto my friend

THROUGHOUT MEDIEVAL TIMES, the betrothal ring was also used as a wedding ring. It is not until the fifteenth century that both a betrothal and wedding ring were given. Historically, men have chosen not to wear wedding rings; it was not until the popularity of the gimmal ring in the sixteenth century that they began to embrace the idea. Double-ring ceremonies became fashionable in the United States during World War II, as the ring became a tangible link to home for young husbands posted overseas. The custom has endured to the present.

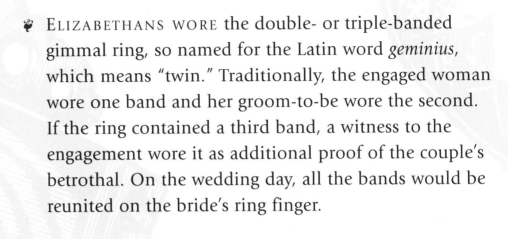

❧ ELIZABETHANS WORE the double- or triple-banded gimmal ring, so named for the Latin word *geminius*, which means "twin." Traditionally, the engaged woman wore one band and her groom-to-be wore the second. If the ring contained a third band, a witness to the engagement wore it as additional proof of the couple's betrothal. On the wedding day, all the bands would be reunited on the bride's ring finger.

❧ RENOWNED FOR THEIR LOVE of poetry and flowers, the Elizabethans exchanged poesy rings with mottoes or poetic love couplets known as poesies engraved on the inside or outside of the band.

❧ USUALLY HANDED DOWN from mother to daughter in Ireland, the Claddagh ring features two hands holding a crowned heart. The crown is worn so that it points toward the wrist on betrothal; upon marriage, the wearer turns the ring around so that the crown faces outward.

❧ THE CELTIC LOVE-KNOT RING, a symbol of eternity, unity, and fidelity, is made of intertwined, unending lines.

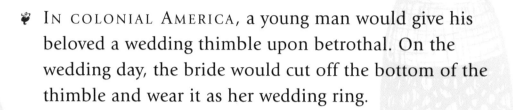

 IN COLONIAL AMERICA, a young man would give his beloved a wedding thimble upon betrothal. On the wedding day, the bride would cut off the bottom of the thimble and wear it as her wedding ring.

 IN FRANCE, it is customary to engrave the bride's name and half of the wedding date on one wedding band and the groom's name and the other half of the date on the other ring. The names and wedding date then come together as the rings are slipped onto the finger during the ceremony.

 IN THE 1870s, Tiffany & Co. designed the first ring with the tone set above the band. This famous Tiffany setting has come to epitomize the modern engagement ring.

 AN OLD IRISH TRADITION had the man presenting his intended with a woven bracelet of human hair as a symbol of his unending love.

 VICTORIANS LOVED to spell messages with gemstones in their rings. For example, **Ruby**, **Emerald**, **Garnet**, **Amethyst**, **Ruby**, **Diamond** says "regard," while **Lapis lazuli**, **Opal**, **Verde** antique, **Emerald** spells "love."

For years my wedding ring
has done its job. It has led me
not into temptation. It has
reminded my husband
numerous times at parties
that it's time to go home.
It has been a source of relief
to a dinner companion.
It has been a status symbol in
the maternity ward.

ERMA BOMBECK

Julia, I bring
To thee this ring,
  Made for thy finger fit;
To show by this
That our love is
  Or should be, like to it.

Loose though it be,
The joint is free;
  So, when love's yoke is on,
It must not gall,
Nor fret at all,
  With hard oppression.

But it must play,
Still either way,
  And be, too, such a yoke
As not too wide
To overslide,
  Or be so straight to choke.

So we who bear
This beam, must rear
  Ourselves to such a height
As that the stay
Of either may
  Create the burthen light.

And as this round
Is nowhere found
  To flaw, or else to sever,
So let our love
As endless prove,
  And pure as gold forever.

TO JULIA
Robert Herrick

Diamonds are a girl's best friend

What's in a stone? Fortune or misfortune, depending on whom you ask. The "true blue" SAPPHIRE promises marital happiness. But the unlucky EMERALD spells jealousy for its wearer, unless the bride-to-be is Irish or born in May, in which case emeralds are highly lucky and will strengthen the eyes, too. Many women have shunned PEARLS because they look like oyster's tears and are feared to bring on a weepy marriage. But Asian brides know that pearls not only stop newlywed tears, but also promote good health and marital bliss. Only October-born brides should wear OPALS, otherwise their changing colors foretell a distrustful marriage. The DIAMOND, perhaps the world's most popular engagement gemstone, is quite lucky. Light that reflects off the brilliant stone wards off jealous evil spirits. For those interested in becoming parents, wearing a diamond will encourage fertility, especially if it touches the skin. Furthermore, wearing a rock that symbolizes eternal and singular love is sure to soothe marital arguments. But the bride who wears an engagement ring with her birthstone may be the luckiest of all.

MONTH	STONE	SYMBOLISM
JANUARY	GARNET	CONSTANCY, FIDELITY
FEBRUARY	AMETHYST	SINCERITY
MARCH	AQUAMARINE	COURAGE
APRIL	DIAMOND	INNOCENCE, PURITY
MAY	EMERALD	HAPPINESS, SUCCESS IN LOVE
JUNE	PEARL	BEAUTY
JULY	RUBY	LOVE, CLARITY OF HEART
AUGUST	PERIDOT	JOY
SEPTEMBER	SAPPHIRE	WISDOM, FAITHFULNESS
OCTOBER	OPAL	CONSISTENCY, FEARLESSNESS
NOVEMBER	TOPAZ	FIDELITY
DECEMBER	TURQUOISE	SUCCESS, PROSPERITY

ENGAGEMENT COCKTAIL PARTY

Often hosted by the bride and groom or their families, a stylish and love-themed cocktail soirée is a simple yet elegant way to celebrate your engagement. Our recipes for champagne punch and delicious heart shaped hors d'oeuvres are the perfect accompaniments for a night of romance. Just add a little Sinatra in the background, tons of candles, some gorgeous flowers and enjoy the moment.

CHAMPAGNE PUNCH

½ cup sugar
1 pineapple, chopped
1 cup fresh lemon juice
1 cup fresh orange juice
2 cups light rum
⅔ cup Cointreau
⅔ cup grenadine
2 bottles champagne, chilled
2 cups ice
Mint leaves and thin orange slices for garnish

1. Combine sugar and pineapple in a large punch bowl. Set aside for 1 hour.

2. Add lemon juice, orange juice, rum, Cointreau and grenadine. Chill for 2 hours.

3. Right before serving add champagne and ice. Garnish each glass with orange slice and mint sprig.

Serves 8-10

LOVELY HORS D'OEUVRES

Delicious and delightful, these sweet heart shaped finger sandwiches are the perfect accompaniment to the Champagne punch. For the toast, we recommend using a loaf of Italian bread (Ciabatta is good) from any gourmet deli, though regular sandwich bread will work, as well. Prepare bite-sized toasts as instructed below and serve with any one of our suggested toppings, or use a favorite recipe of your own.

MINI HEART SHAPED TOASTS

3 loaves white bread
extra virgin olive oil
small heart shaped
cookie cutter

Thinly slice the bread and cut out heart shapes with the cookie cutter. Arrange the individual hearts on a baking sheet, drizzle with olive oil, and toast until golden brown. Toasts may be made up to one day in advance and stored in an airtight container at room temperature.

Makes approximately 120 small heart shaped toasts. (Quantity will vary depending on size of cookie cutter and bread loaf.)

CAVIAR TOPPING

6 tablespoons
crème fraiche

2 ounces
high quality caviar

Thinly spread crème fraiche on heart toasts and top with a small dollop of caviar. Keep covered until ready to serve.

Makes approximately 40 Caviar Toasts.

CHOPPED TOMATO AND PARMESAN TOPPING

4 large tomatoes, chopped

1 red onion, chopped

4 tablespoons olive oil

2 teaspoon fresh basil, finely chopped

4 teaspoons fresh parsley, finely chopped

1/2 cup freshly grated Parmesan cheese

salt and pepper to taste

1. In a large bowl, combine tomatoes, onion, olive oil, basil, parsley, salt and pepper.

2. Place heart toasts on baking sheet and top with tomato mixture. Sprinkle with Parmesan cheese.

3. Broil for 2-3 minutes or until Parmesan cheese has completely melted. Cool for 3-5 minutes and serve warm.

Makes approximately 40 Tomato and Parmesan Toasts.

MUSHROOM AND GOAT'S CHEESE TOPPING

10 medium sized field mushrooms, sliced

4 tablespoons butter

1 red chili, finely diced

2 shallot, finely chopped

4 cloves of garlic, crushed

sprig of fresh thyme, finely chopped

1/2 lb crumbled goat's cheese

salt and pepper to taste

1. In medium sized sauté pan, melt butter. Add shallots, chili, garlic, thyme and mushrooms. Sauté on high heat until mushrooms and shallots are soft.

2. Place heart toasts on baking sheet and top with mushroom mixture. Sprinkle with goat's cheese.

3. Broil for 2-3 minutes or until Parmesan cheese has completely melted and just started to brown. Cool for 3-5 minutes and serve warm.

Makes approximately 40 Mushroom and Goats Cheese Toasts.

Marry when the year is new.
Always loving, kind and true.
When February birds do mate
You may wed, nor dread your fate.
If you wed when March winds blow,
Joy and sorrow both you'll know.
Marry in April when you can,
Joy for maiden and for man.
Marry in the month of May
You will surely rue the day.
Marry when June roses blow,
Over land and sea you'll go.
Those who in July do wed
Labor always for their bread.
Whoever wed in August be
Many a change is sure to see.
Marry in September's shrine
Your living will be rich and fine.
If in October you do marry,
Love will come but riches tarry.
If you wed in bleak November
Only joy will come, remember.
When December's snows fall fast,
Marry and true love will last.

GROOM'S GIFT: THE BOOK OF US

12–24 sheets of 8 ½" x 11" lightweight card stock, 2 sheets of 9" x 11 ½" heavy-weight card stock, two pieces of 9 ½" x 11 ½" decorative fabric or leather, hole punch, scissors, craft glue, 1–2 yards of ribbon or leather cord, various colored or handmade papers, vellum or cellophane, self-adhesive photo corners

YOUR FIRST TOOTH, his first step, your bad teenage hair days, his class picture, your first date together, his first bouquet of flowers to you, your first love letter to him. You can display your early years apart and relive the romantic memories of how your lives came together in a special scrapbook that preserves the keepsakes of your past and your present, while allowing adequate space for your future. Surprise your fiancé by having it delivered to him on the morning of your wedding.

❧ Buy an album-style blank book from your local stationer or follow these simple instructions to make your own:

❧ Cut a dozen or so pages of lightweight card stock paper to the desired length and width of your scrapbook. Use a hole punch to create two or three holes along the short side of the pages.

- To make the front and back cover for your scrapbook, cut two pages of heavyweight card stock about a ¼ inch wider and longer than your inside pages. Then cut two rectangles of fabric or leather about ½ inch wider than your cover pieces. Brush craft glue on one side of each piece and cover with fabric. Fold the edges of the fabric on the other side and glue in place. After the glue has dried, punch holes in the front and back covers to line up with the inside pages.

- To bind the book, string lengths of ribbon, cord, or leather through the holes and tie a knot and bow.

- Conspire with your fiancé's family to get photographs of his cutest (and most embarrassing!) moments *pre-you,* and dig through your family archives to find photographic evidence of your own similar moments.

- Gather together movie stubs, tickets and programs from sports and entertainment events, menus from favorite restaurants, labels from special bottles of wine, romantic notes, letters and postcards, pressed flowers, ribbons, a selection of photographs, and other mementos from your dating days.

- Arrange your graphic timelines side by side chronologically in the order you want to display them in your scrapbook.

- Using craft glue and old-fashioned photo corners, affix your momentos to the pages of your scrapbook. Add hand-written captions including dates and descriptions.

- To make pockets in your scrapbook for your courtship memories, cut various-sized squares of card stock. Create an aesthetic look with opaque or colored paper, handmade paper, or paper made with flower petals. Glue or sew paper squares in place along the bottom and side edges. For see-through pockets, try using vellum or heavyweight cellophane. Affix small envelopes with glue in your scrapbook to store love letters or poems. Begin the scrapbook with a private letter to your fiancé, to be read the morning of your wedding.

- If you wish to add to your scrapbook once you are married, just add pages and replace ribbons with longer pieces, if necessary.

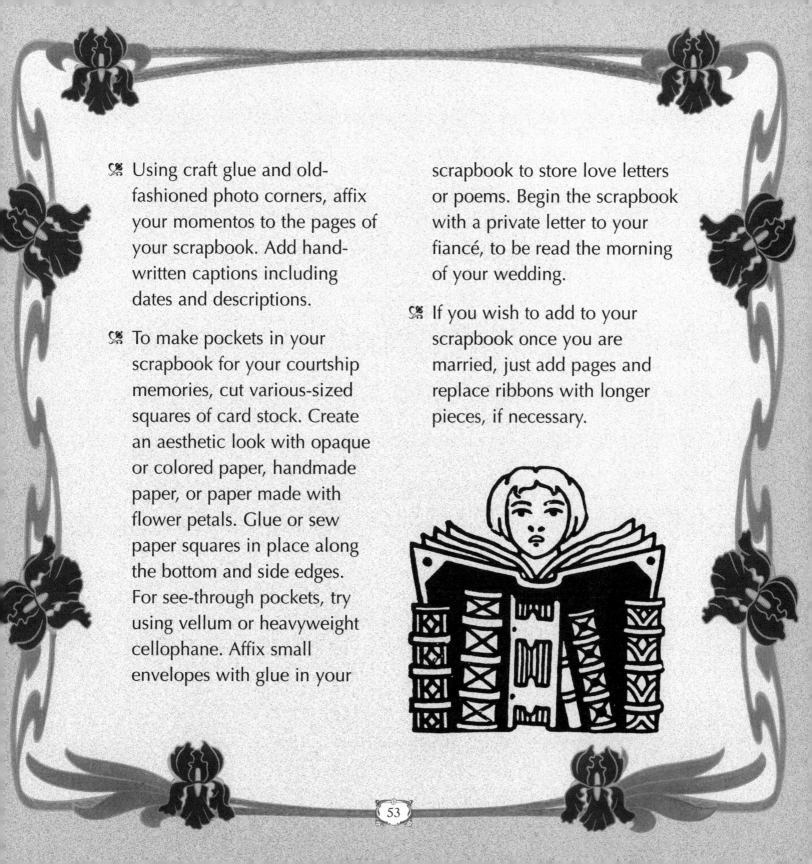

To keep your marriage brimming,

With love in the loving cup,

Whenever you're wrong, admit it;

Whenever you're right, shut up.

Ogden Nash

Thanks to a love-struck Dutch maiden, modern brides are showered with gifts and surprises before they are wed. According to folklore, the custom began some three hundred years ago when the daughter of a well-to-do Dutchman fell in love with a miller. He was a good man, but her father disapproved, for the miller was poor from giving flour away to the less fortunate. When the bride's father refused to give his daughter a dowry, her friends and neighbors showered her with enough gifts and blessings so that she could marry her true love after all.

Showering the bride

Ever since, friends of brides-to-be regularly descend upon the bride and load her with advice, good luck, and presents that will start her off in her new home and new life. In the 1890s, it became fashionable to place gifts for the new bride into a Japanese parasol. Later the bride was "showered" with presents as the parasol was opened over her head. Another popular Victorian container for shower gifts was a crepe-paper wishing well.

THROUGHOUT EUROPE AND AFRICA, brides have commonly packed a trousseau, or "bottom drawer," filled with linens, clothing, and jewels. Neighbors in colonial America frequently gathered for a quilting bee, an all-day event during which they'd sew a quilt with a double wedding ring or other nuptial pattern. In Lithuania, the night before the wedding, the bride's closest friends bestow her with handwoven articles and spend the night helping her pack her hope chest. Many elder African village women will "load the bride" with words of wisdom and household goods.

SHOWERS OFTEN COME AS A SURPRISE to the bride, who can expect to be subjected to a fair amount of good-natured fun and games. Gift givers who know that each broken ribbon foretells a baby might go out of their way to wrap presents with extra ties and tape to make sure the bride will have to cut or rip them. In times past, a bridesmaid might have gathered all the ribbons into a pillow to keep in the newlyweds' home for continual good luck. Now a bridesmaid often ties all the ribbons together into a mock bouquet to use during the wedding rehearsal.

A Hurry of Showers

GREEN THUMB: An informal picnic luncheon where guests shower the bride with garden tools, seeds, bulbs, plants, and garden ornaments. Guests may also plant a bridal wreath for the lucky couple.

NEST BUILDER: Fill the bride's linen closets with tablecloths, lace napkins, napkin holders, towels, place mats, bed sheets, duvet covers, pillows, and pillowcases.

AROUND THE WORLD: Each guest is assigned a country and then brings a gift reflecting that culture. For example, Italy might buy a pasta maker or pizza stone; Japan, a wok or cookbook; and England, a set of teacups and fine teas.

'ROUND THE CLOCK: Assign each guest a time of day on the invitation and inform them that the gift they choose should correspond to that time—7 A.M. could be an alarm clock or bathroom accessories; 10 A.M. might be a coffeemaker or coffee mugs; lunchtime, cooking utensils or a salad bowl; bedtime, lingerie or linens, etc.

EVENING OF BEAUTY & BLISS: Guests bring candles, beauty products, spa certificates, and even classic movies for an evening of soothing music, soft aromatic candlelight, and spa fare—designed to help the bride feel relaxed, pampered, and beautiful.

RECIPE ROUND-UP: A potluck lunch or dinner where each guest brings a special dish, its recipe, and a gift to help stock the bride's kitchen. Include a blank recipe card with the invitation then collect the filled-in cards into a recipe box at the shower.

As a young girl growing up in Cleveland, Ohio, I was especially enchanted by Grandmother Barkin's most cherished possession, a quilt she had made with swatches from the wedding gowns of generations of brides in our family.

When company would come for tea, Grandmother would spread out the quilt, enthralling her guests and especially me with her tales of each delicate piece and the bride who wore it. The well-to-do brides in our family left behind swatches

GRANDMOTHER'S QUILT
RETOLD FROM A STORY BY ANNIE F. S. BEARD

of silk, satin, brocade, and velvet, while the pioneer brides of lesser means contributed their soft muslin and calico. A piece from Grandmother's own wedding gown was proudly displayed in the center of the quilt, where she had embroidered "Love One Another" atop the fading blue satin.

To my delight, Grandmother would often smile sweetly and say, "This wedding quilt will be yours one day, dear Mary." Since Grandmother had only sons and no daughter and I was the eldest granddaughter, the quilt would be passed down to me if I married first.

Although I was approaching twenty-five, I was more concerned with the kind of man I wanted to marry than getting married just for the sake of getting married. I sincerely doubted I would ever own the quilt until my childhood friend Leonard Wynn and I began to take the same path to work each day.

As Leonard and I would wind our way through the narrow streets leading to town, he would amuse me with his stories. However, one crisp fall day in 1861 any hope of our romance developing was dashed when he informed me he had enlisted in the Union army. When the day came to see him off at the train station, I felt as though my heart would break.

The enthusiasm and patriotic spirit of the women of Cleveland reached a zenith during the Civil War. And Grandmother Barkin and I were no exception. Freely and abundantly Grandmother sent supplies from her stores. But her crowning sacrifice was yet to be made.

Early one bright winter morning a carriage rolled up to Grandmother's door, and out of it stepped two eager young ladies who took Grandmother aside and said in whispered tones, "So you see, Mrs. Barkin, we are desperate for quilts for our soldiers." Slowly rising from her chair, the elderly lady stood and then proceeded to her wardrobe. Out came her treasured quilt, wrapped in white and fragrant with lavender. Calling to me, she said, "Mary, they need quilts at the hospital. I have no other ready-made ones. Are you willing to give this one up?"

I hesitated for only a moment, realizing that every gift added one more chance of comfort for my Leonard.

So Grandmother's quilt adorned one of the cots in the hospital and gave warmth and pleasure to many a poor sufferer, serving a purpose far greater than its maker had intended.

Grandmother and I joined the tireless group at the Cleveland hospital. One Christmas as I was passing from cot to cot distributing grapes and oranges, I watched the eager looks of the poor fellows. Having emptied my basket, I went to assist in feeding those who were unable to help themselves.

Taking a plate of jelly in my hand, I stepped to the side of one of the cots, noticing as I did that Grandmother's quilt lay upon the bed! The sight of it brought a rush of tender memories, filling my eyes with tears so that for a moment I didn't see the face upon the pillow.

Then, with a start, I saw Leonard Wynn. As I dried my eyes, I got a closer look at the white face with sunken eyes revealing the depth of his pain. "No, it can't be," I assured myself.

But the familiar voice erased all doubt. "Ah, Mary, I've been watching and waiting for you!"

Overjoyed I asked, "Why didn't you send for me?"

"I knew you would come sometime. The sight of this," he said, touching the quilt, "made me sure of it."

During the next few weeks, we rediscovered the joys of our companionship. That happiness was quickly extinguished, however, when I arrived at the hospital early one morning to find Leonard's bed occupied by another wounded soldier. A nurse informed me that Leonard had returned to his regiment. Along with Leonard, Grandmother's quilt had also vanished. And so, the Christmas of 1862 came and went, bringing with it joyous surprise only to snatch it and Grandmother's quilt away.

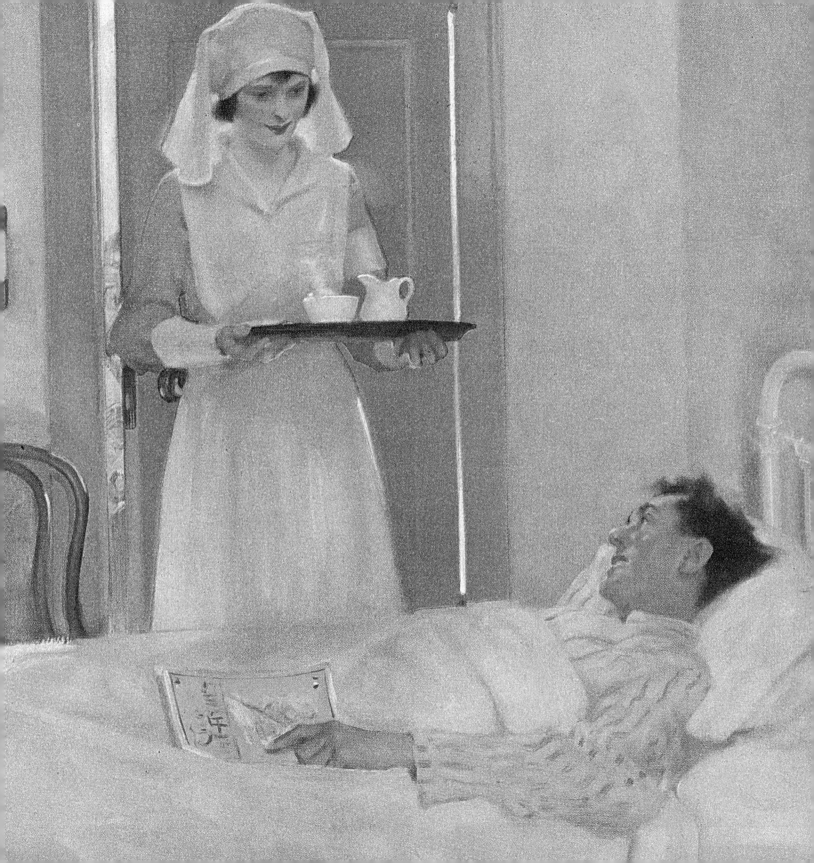

Another long year passed. I was as busy as ever, assisting the cause by trying to impart the Christmas spirit to the soldiers in the hospital. One evening at the close of the day's proceedings, I wearily laid my head down on a table. It was quickly growing dark, and I closed my eyes to snatch, if possible, a brief interval of much needed rest.

Suddenly I was startled. How long had I been asleep, and what was this lying under my head? One glance revealed Grandmother's quilt. How did it get there? I squealed with delight as I heard a familiar voice— Leonard's. "I've come for my Christmas gift, sweet Mary," he said as he drew the quilt to his chest and pointed to the inscription, "Love one another." "I wanted to ask you a year ago but decided that I would not ask you to take a maimed, sick soldier. I kept the quilt in memory of you. See, I fixed it so it would come back to you if anything happened to me." He showed me the label fastened securely to the quilt: "To be sent to Miss Mary Barkin, Cleveland, Ohio."

Then he told me how on one cold winter's day the quilt had saved his life. While sitting close to the fire to warm himself and to cook some potatoes, a stray ball from the enemy's batteries came whistling through the air, taking a straight course toward him. Luckily he was wrapped in the quilt. The ball struck him but, because of the thickness of the quilt, got no further than his coat.

That night Grandmother's quilt went back to its original owner, and my right to it as a wedding gift was firmly established by Leonard's proposal.

*F*rom head to toe, virtually every accessory the bride wears on her wedding day is rife with superstition. Here are some age-old ways women have secured their good luck on the way to the altar:

Something old, something new, something borrowed,

WHEN A BRIDE wears something old, such as an heirloom, it's a link to her family roots. Something new is a show of optimism about what is to come. The good fortune of a happily married woman is sure to rub off on a new bride when she wears borrowed jewels or accessories.

THE COLOR BLUE is a symbol of purity and fidelity, according to the Old Testament. Ancient Israelites were among the first to wear blue on wedding days.

TO WEAR A VEIL is certain to shield the bride from the Evil Eye. Many African brides have their hair braided to be worn as a veil.

GREEK BRIDES tuck a sugar cube inside a glove to ensure sweetness throughout marriage.

COLONIAL BRIDES carried a small pouch with a coin, a breadcrumb, wood, and cloth to be sure they'd always have money, food, shelter, and clothing.

SWEDISH BRIDES leave their shoes unfastened during their wedding ceremonies in the hopes that childbirth will come easily.

something blue and a silver sixpence in your shoe

TO MAKE SURE they'll never be without happiness or wealth, brides throughout Europe and America slip a coin in their shoes.

A LUCKY HORSESHOE strewn with ribbons is a favored totem of Irish brides.

The best and
most beautiful
things in the
world cannot
be seen or
even touched.
They must
be felt with
the heart.

HELEN KELLER

A ROOM WITH A VIEW

E. M. FORSTER

"YOU MUST MARRY, or your life will be wasted. You have gone too far to retreat. I have no time for the tenderness, and the comradeship, and the poetry, and the things that really matter, and *for which* you marry. I know that, with George, you will find them and that you love him. Then be his wife. He is already part of you. Though you fly to Greece, and never see him again, or forget his very name, George will work in your thoughts till you die. It isn't possible to love and to part. You will wish that it was. You can transmute love, ignore it, muddle it, but you can never pull it out of you…love is eternal….

"I only wish poets would say this, too: love is of the body; not the body but of the body. Ah! the misery that would be saved if we confessed that!…When I think what life is, and how seldom love is answered by love— Marry him; it is one of the moments for which the world was made…."

On your wedding day, beauty and flowers will surround you. Your dearest friends and relatives, your personal "ladies in waiting," will lavish their attention upon you alone. If you're having a traditional wedding, you'll probably deck your bridesmaids out in matching gowns that complement the style and décor of the big event. But just how did this custom of look-alike bridesmaids originate?

Always a bridesmaid, never a bride

IN THE WESTERN TRADITION, the practice of surrounding the bride with similarly dressed young women started as a defense against the bride-stealing Anglo-Saxon and Germanic marauders. The earliest bridesmaids often dressed identically to the bride, in the same color gowns—including veils—to act as decoys and confuse potential kidnappers.

WHAT OF THE GROOM'S BEST MAN? In days of yore, he was generally the right-hand man of the thieving tribesman, ready to assist in snatching the unsuspecting "bride elect." Additional comrades ensured a successful raid for the groom and, if they were lucky, might steal a bride of their own.

IT WAS ALSO ONCE BELIEVED that surrounding the bride with a flock of bridesmaids would ward off harmful spirits who might place a curse on the bride and groom's happiness. Early Greek maidens often wed at age fifteen, and tradition called for these young brides to be escorted by a train of happily married, fertile women who served the dual purpose of protecting the bride from evil and allowing their own good fortune to rub off on her.

IN SOME CASES, bridal parties took extreme measures, dressing like men to protect themselves against misfortune. In Denmark, the bride and groom changed sex roles to ensure a successful wedding. One ancient Jewish tradition called for the bride to be clad in full armor, complete with helmet and weaponry.

ATTENDANT GIFTS

THEY'LL STAND BY YOUR SIDE through tears and laughter and make certain you look radiant on your wedding day. It's only natural for you to do something special for your attendants to thank them for all their support and comfort during your engagement and wedding. The custom of the bride bestowing gifts on her bridesmaids is centuries old. Traditionally, the bride paid for the gloves her attendants wore during the ceremony. Nowadays, the bride might give her bridesmaids jewelry or hair accessories that they can wear on the wedding day. Whether you choose classic or modern gifts will depend on what you think your attendants will appreciate most.

For a personal touch, consider giving your bridesmaids a handmade gift they can use for your wedding and many occasions to come. Handkerchief purses are easy to sew and an elegant way to say thank you. Begin by looking for antique handkerchiefs or linen napkins with embroidered borders or lace trim. Choose complementary decorative ribbons to use as handles.

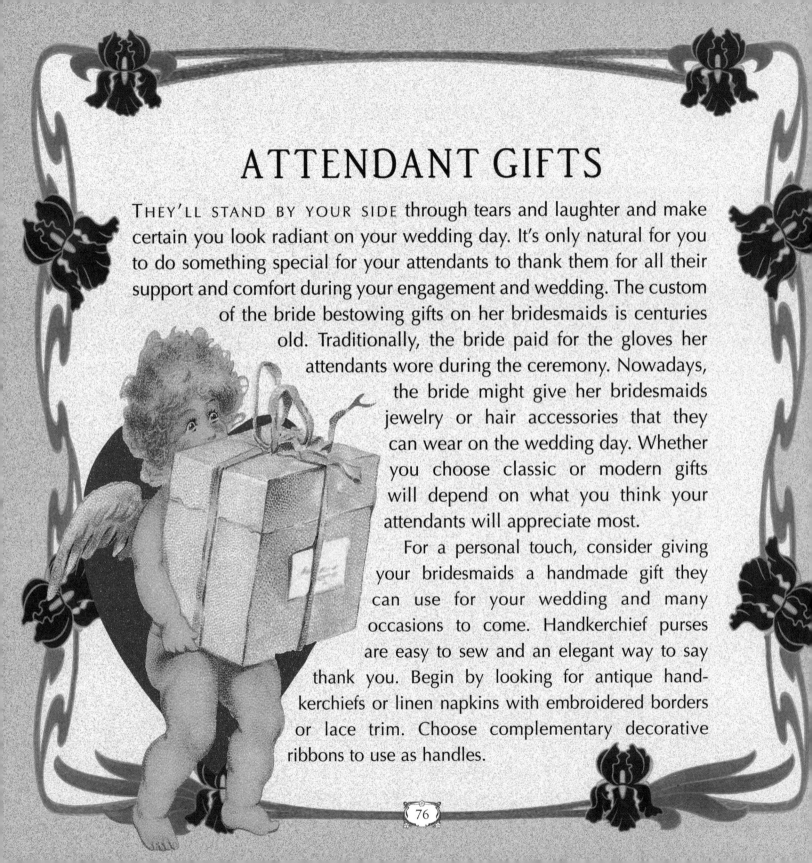

HANDMADE HANDKERCHIEF PURSE

Antique handkerchief or linen napkin, thread, pins, 18-inch length of satin ribbon

1. Starch and press handkerchief.

2. Lay handkerchief wrong side down and fold the bottom half up to meet the top edge. Pin the sides together.

3. Sew the sides by machine or by hand with a backstitch.

4. Pin ribbon ends to the inside seams and sew in place.

5. Turn the bag inside out and press.

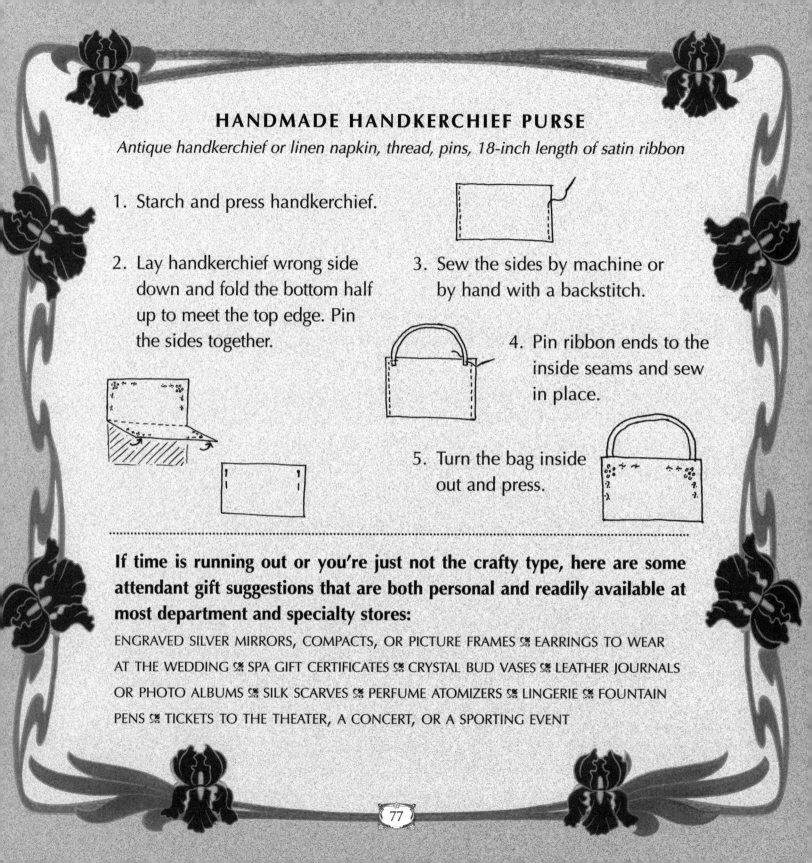

If time is running out or you're just not the crafty type, here are some attendant gift suggestions that are both personal and readily available at most department and specialty stores:

ENGRAVED SILVER MIRRORS, COMPACTS, OR PICTURE FRAMES ❦ EARRINGS TO WEAR AT THE WEDDING ❦ SPA GIFT CERTIFICATES ❦ CRYSTAL BUD VASES ❦ LEATHER JOURNALS OR PHOTO ALBUMS ❦ SILK SCARVES ❦ PERFUME ATOMIZERS ❦ LINGERIE ❦ FOUNTAIN PENS ❦ TICKETS TO THE THEATER, A CONCERT, OR A SPORTING EVENT

BRIDAL TEA PARTY

In the busy days before your wedding, hosting a "girls only" bridesmaids' luncheon can be a welcome break for you and your attendants. Such occasions are ideal opportunities to thank your bridesmaids with individual gifts and an appetizing array of food. The menu for a bridal tea includes finger sandwiches and salads, most of which can be prepared a day ahead. In addition to an assortment of teas, you may want to offer sherry or champagne cocktails.

A mismatched tea set is a charming option for an informal luncheon, and if you plan to serve several different kinds of tea, you'll be using different pots anyway! Rifle through antique shops, flea markets, thrift stores, and sales at home and department stores for a variety of pretty, quality teapots, teacups, and saucers with no cracks. After lunch, wash and pack all the cups and saucers (don't forget to have some newspaper or tissue paper handy) and present each bridesmaid with one as a souvenir.

MENU SUGGESTIONS

TEA SERVICE

assorted loose black and herbal teas
cinnamon sticks
lemon and orange slices
honey
sugar cubes
cream and milk

To make the perfect pot of tea, start with cold, freshly drawn water. Bring water to a rolling boil and immediately pour a small amount in the teapot. Swirl the hot water around to warm the teapot, then discard. Place one teaspoon of tea leaves per cup of water into the teapot, then pour the water over the leaves. Steep for 3 to 5 minutes. Pour tea through a small strainer to serve.

FINGER SANDWICHES

cucumber & cream cheese
tomato & herbed butter
salmon, cream cheese, & dill
watercress & cream cheese
thinly sliced turkey & Dijon mustard-cranberry sauce spread
prosciutto & melon slices
aged cheddar & tomato

Remove the crusts from an assortment of light and dark slices of bread. Spread with herbed butter or cream cheese and various toppings. Then halve or quarter the slices to make bite-size tea sandwiches.

SWEET TREATS

fresh fruit salad
shortbread
currant scones
lemon poundcake
petit fours

A proper high tea always includes something sweet to balance the savory. If you include breakfast breads, be sure to offer butter and strawberry jam.

CHARM CAKE

Treat your attendants to a sweet slice of fortune with their tea and bake a Victorian-style bridesmaids' cake embedded with silver charms attached to long ribbons. According to lore, the bride should sift the flour with her own hands to infuse the cake with her good luck. Before the cake is cut, each bridesmaid pulls a ribbon to discover what future her charm predicts. Shop local yard sales and jewelry stores for inexpensive silver charms.

Typical Charms and Their Meanings:

airplane = travel

anchor = life of stability

baby buggy = children

clover = good luck

flowers = blossoming love

heart = true love will find you

key = happy home

knot = steadfast love

money tree = life of riches

ring = next engaged

rocking chair = long life

telephone = good news

wishing well = granted wish

wreath = contented life

FOR CAKE:

1 stick (½ cup) butter

1 ¼ cups sugar

1 cup milk

1 tablespoon vanilla

2 ¼ cups pastry flour

2 ½ teaspoons baking powder

¼ teaspoon salt

4 egg whites

1. Preheat oven to 375° F.

2. In large bowl, cream butter and sugar until light and fluffy. Add milk and vanilla and mixed until blended.

3. In separate bowl, sift flour, baking powder, and salt. Add to wet mixture in thirds. After each addition, stir the batter until smooth.

4. Whip egg whites until stiff. Fold into batter.

5. Pour batter evenly into two greased 9-inch round cake pans. Bake for about 25 minutes or until tester comes out clean. Allow to cool completely on racks before frosting.

FOR ICING:

1 stick (½ cup) unsalted butter

3 ½ cups confectioner's sugar

3 tablespoons whipping cream

1 lemon rind, grated

½ teaspoon orange extract

1. In medium bowl, cream butter and sugar together until smooth.

2. Beat in whipping cream.

3. Add lemon rind and orange extract and mix until blended.

4. With a spatula, spread icing on top of first layer of cake. Stack second layer on top and spread remaining icing over sides of cake.

5. Arrange charms evenly around the top layer of cake. Gently press charms into the cake with your fingertip. Then carefully ice the top of the cake, leaving ribbons exposed.

Tip: To prevent ribbons from getting iced while you work, wrap them in plastic wrap or aluminum foil. Remove the wrap prior to serving.

Go seek her out all courteously,
And say I come,
Wind of spices whose song is ever
Epithalamium.
O hurry over the dark lands
And run upon the sea
For seas and land shall not divide us
My love and me.

Now, wind, of your good courtesy
I pray you go,
And come into her little garden
And sing at her window;
Singing: The bridal wind is blowing
For Love is at his noon;
And soon will your true love be with you,
Soon, O soon.

POEM XIII FROM *CHAMBER MUSIC*
James Joyce

On her wedding day, the bride leaves behind her old life, ready to embark upon her new status as a married woman. To bridge that transition, cultures throughout the world partake in cleansing and beautifying rituals that start the bride off on the right foot. Many such customs are performed with the aid of married women, with the belief that their good fortune will rub off on the new bride.

Preparing the bride for her walk down the aisle

BODY ART

As part of several days of premarital preparation, Moroccan and Egyptian women immerse themselves in specially prepared milk baths and have body hair removed with a homemade lemon-sugar depilatory recipe. They, as well as Muslim women in India, Nigeria, and Ethiopia, are treated to full-body massages with coconut or olive oil. Finally, professional henna artists paint their hands and feet with elaborate designs. The artwork lasts for several days and is believed to keep malevolent spirits at bay.

In other parts of the world, brides have their faces adorned to greet their new husbands. Korean women have red dots painted on their cheeks and foreheads. Masai women decorate their faces and hair with red ocher dye. And in Indonesia, brides are beautified with patterns of white dots on their cheeks, noses, and foreheads.

RITUAL BATH

In China, the day before her wedding, a bride takes a purifying herbal bath prepared with bamboo, pine, and the pungent herb artemisia, so that her married life may be long, prosperous, and strong. Young Jewish women partake in a special bath called a mikvah, in which the elder women of the community participate. The bride to be is immersed several times in a special pool or natural body of water and recites a blessing for spiritual purification. She emerges from the water "born anew" to cross the sacred threshold into marriage. Navaho women also come together to prepare the bride with a ritual bath and help her dress for her nuptials. A Hopi mother will wash her daughter's hair with yucca root to purify her on her wedding day.

FOOD OF LOVE

While American brides typically lose weight in preparation for their wedding day, some brides in Nigeria, Togo, and Tanzania spend weeks eating specially made foods to fatten up so they may be voluptuous, fertile, and beautiful for their new husbands.

Marry when the sun doth shine

Once you spread the news that you're getting married, most everyone will have a bit of advice about what ensures good luck on the Big Day. If you find a spider on your wedding gown, you'll come into money. If you marry on the incoming tide, you'll have prosperity. If you see a flock of birds, your marriage will be blessed with fertility. If it snows, you'll be wealthy. If the sun is out, you'll be a happy bride. These tried-and-true Old Wives' tales may help you garner all the luck possible on your wedding day.

DO

- ❧ Marry under a waxing moon so happiness will grow.

- ❧ Marry as the hands of the clock move up (after the half hour) for good fortune.

- ❧ Throw away all the pins from your bridal wear after the wedding for a long marriage.

and you'll be a happy bride

DON'T

- ❧ Wear the complete wedding attire before the wedding day.

- ❧ Look in the mirror before walking down the aisle, lest you leave any part of yourself behind.

- ❧ Allow the groom to see you in your dress before the wedding. It's bad luck to see the future before it happens.

- ❧ Drop the ring during the ceremony, or else it's best to start over.

- ❧ Wear the wedding ring before the wedding day.

- ❧ Shed tears before the kiss. To cry on your wedding day prevents tears during the marriage.

- ❧ Invite an even number of guests to attend the ceremony.

- ❧ Feed a cat out of your wedding shoe for good luck.

- ❧ Kiss a chimney sweep if you see one on your wedding day. You'll have good luck throughout your marriage.

- ❧ Sew a penny into the seam of your wedding dress for luck on your wedding day and prosperity in your wedded life.

THE PAMPERED BRIDE

On her wedding day, a bride deserves to look and feel like a queen. Treat yourself to an at-home spa in the days leading up to your wedding to bring out your most beautiful self. Try these easy steps to overnight radiance.

- Soak away pre-wedding tension with a bath of Epsom salts and lavender. Add 3 cups of Epsom salts and 1 cup finely ground lavender buds to a bath of warm water. Exfoliate with a body brush and finish off by massaging coconut oil into your skin for ultimate softness.

- Revive fatigued and sensitive skin with rose water. Boil a white rose and gently rub the petals into your face until the moisture vaporizes. Or, treat yourself to a facial by mixing 2 tablespoons rose water, 2 tablespoons yogurt, 1 tablespoon honey, and 2 tablespoons dried rose petals and lavender, crumbled. Dab the mixture onto your face and relax. After 20 minutes, rinse and pat dry.

- Make your lips even more kissable with a soft-bristled toothbrush. Gently brush your lips to rub away dry or dead skin and leave them ever so smooth.

- Soothe your dry eyes with the cooling properties of cucumber. A few hydrating slices on your eyes really do help hide delicate lines. When tears of joy leave your eyes red and puffy, calm them with moistened chamomile tea bags.

- Give yourself shiny, voluminous hair with a protein-packed egg and avocado conditioner. Mix one egg and half of an avocado and massage into hair and scalp. Leave in for at least 20 minutes before rinsing.

- Your overworked hands deserve some special attention for the moment your groom places your wedding band on your finger. Blend 1 tablespoon honey, 1 tablespoon almond oil, and $3/4$ teaspoon lemon juice. Rub the mixture into your skin and rest for

STRESS-FREE EMERGENCY PACK
Avoid last-minute mishaps by preparing a basket in the bridal suite for you and your bridesmaids. Include:

ASPIRIN ❧ BAND-AIDS ❧ CHALK OR WHITE MEDICAL TAPE (FOR HIDING SMUDGES ON WHITE FABRIC) ❧ CLEAR NAIL POLISH (FOR SNAGGED HOSIERY) ❧ COMPACT POWDER ❧ EMERY BOARD ❧ GUM OR MINTS ❧ HAIRBRUSH ❧ HAIR SPRAY ❧ LIPSTICK OR LIP BALM ❧ LOTION ❧ NEEDLE & THREAD ❧ NOTEPAD & PEN ❧ SAFETY PINS ❧ TISSUES

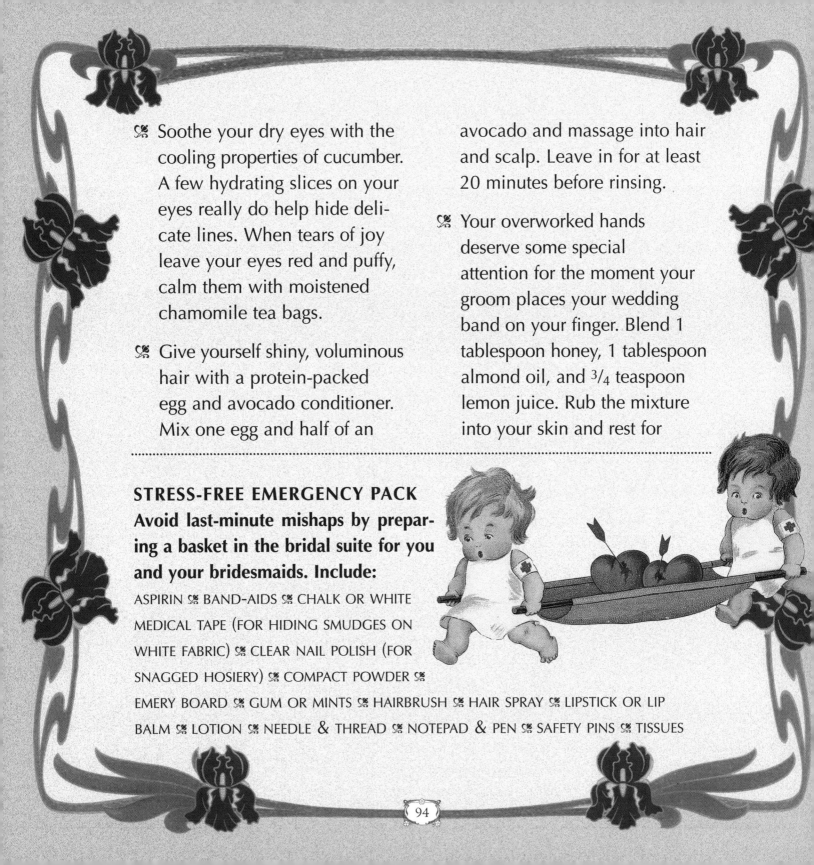

about 10 minutes. Rinse with warm water for soft, sweet-smelling skin.

❦ You'll be standing on them all day long, so give your feet some extra love before you walk down the aisle. Make a heel-to- toe softening foot scrub by mixing 2 cups sea salt, 2 table-spoons dried, chopped orange peel, 3 drops essential oil of lavender, and 3 drops essential oil of tea tree. Gently massage into your feet during a bath or shower.